Musings
and
Meanderings

SKEETER SMITH

Musings and Meanderings copyright © 2026 by Skeeter Smith

First edition, March 2026
ISBN 979-8-9936800-0-2

Formatting by Vision Press

Visit vision-press.com or email visionpressal@gmail.com for more information about self-publishing services or author queries.

Musings
and
Meanderings

Table of Contents

What Others Are Saying

"Who wants a good book of poems that makes you feel like it's your thoughts and your memories? When you start reading it's like visiting with an old friend." — I. Johnson

"I have never been a dreamer but maybe I should…I have always been a spectator of the arts…Intrinsic access to the quality of life this I can understand. Works spoken by you wake up my dreamer. Give me freedom to think and tap in below the surface. I am grateful for your inspiration to allow myself to feel without apology, be who I am and that is enough." — J. Madrid

"Makes the ups and downs of life more tolerable and speaks to resilience."
—J. Anderson

TENDERNESS

THE STORY

I would do it all again

Exactly the same,

Would not change a thing,

Because the struggle is the story.

THOUSAND LIFETIMES

In a thousand lifetimes

I would still have found you

Searched you out.

Knowing in each life

Our paths would cross.

Because you are my eternity

And I am your destiny.

TUMBLEWEEDS

Tumbleweed, tumbleweeds

Blowing through my past,

Reminding me of desert drifters

Brown sprigs were once grass.

Tumbling across my vision

Promising to land,

Nothing but blowing,

Nothing but sand.

8

SILENCE

Silence exists in gentle repose

Listening to forever

Because you told me…

It was so.

JOYFUL MOMENTS

Joyful moments

Tiny blips of time,

An instant of infinite gladness

Crosses my mind.

Perfect moments

One at a time,

Come to me seldom.

Sustainable moments

Keeping them on queue,

Ready at the memory.

Heartfelt moments

Recalling the time

Present in that minute.

Sunshine moments

Feeling in the air

Watchful, forever memory.

Blissful, simple moments

Zen whispering in the wind,

Forever on my mind

Imbued on my soul.

LOVING YOU IS EASY

Loving you is easy

Nothing to it at all,

The simplest kind of gentleness

Gives meaning to the years.

Loving me is easy

Recalling the tears,

Struggling was the message

Giving meaning to my tears.

Taking time for memories

Wasn't so bad at all,

I know the message and struggle

Created meaning for my soul.

Taking time for memories

So hard on me,

So easy to pass judgment

So hard to be tender.

Tender and gentle

Compassion for me,

Not easy to get there

Not so simple

Even for me.

THE FEELING

A funny kind of feeling

One you just cannot shake,

When you know something is out there

Just won't show its face.

My mind wanders

Wondering what it means

To not put a finger on it,

Makes the space easier to comprehend.

Doesn't really matter

No definition at all,

Just let it be there

The answers will follow.

Understanding the message

Doesn't mean you need to know it all.

CASTAWAY

Nobody gets you

A castaway-

Flirting from dandelion to dandelion

Blowing white through the air

Flittering in the dusk.

Nobody to catch you

Never finding surface

Each gust

Blowing in the wind.

Clouds scurry by

Casting shadows over light

Shining through,

Brief respite

Throwing it all awry.

Like a chewed-up piece of gum

Lost the sugar

Discarding remnants of a once great taste

Memories cannot find you.

GOD'S MUSE

A MOTHER'S LOVE

A mother's love

Prerequisite to all I've learned in this life

Taught in the home.

A beacon of silence,

Unconditional nurturing

Lives forever in the heart

Never ending.

My best teacher; my mother.

My best lesson; my daughter.

My forever compassion

Life altering experience.

A mother's love is eternal,

An everlasting love

A generational love

Beams into my heart

And makes me whole.

MOTHERS

Blessed are our mothers who create, sustain and endure.

Who feed the needy, adopt the motherless, and nurture along the way.

Mother, grandmother, aunt, sister, dog mom, kitty mom, indefensible,

The reason life continues.

Because you are mom in so many ways, creator of worlds, and creator of love.

Mother...you are the life and air I continue to breathe.

PICTURES OF YOU

I keep pictures of you

To remind me

The only real thing

To bless my life.

The meaningful bits

Amongst noisy obligations.

Pictures tell my story

Pictures I took of you.

Now survived by memory

Seared into my eyes.

My best piece poetry,

My pictures of you.

I GOT NEWS FOR YOU

I got news for you

This is what a mother does.

You say she is controlling

Her only purpose is to love.

Finding that delicate balance

A lifetime of mothering

A lifetime investment.

You grow older,

As does she,

But her heart is always tender

Looking after your needs.

She will never stop controlling.

She will never stop the bossy,

Because she is your mother

That is her job.

GRANDKIDS

Ruby is sunshine,

River is joy,

Ruth is the cupcake,

Sprinkles me with more.

Grandkids are my purpose,

Daisies all galore

God's tiny sprits

Showering me with more.

MIDDLE CHILD

The inevitable part of middle child

Caught in birth order

And in between.

Requires extra compassion

And timeless affection

Living in the middle.

A combination of three

A tiny bit of extra

A love so gentle.

She innately understands

The balance of the three.

Looks to approval

While pulling back to 'me'.

BABY OF THE FAMILY

My sisters say I'm the favorite

I would disagree.

Fourth daughter

Baby of the family.

Our dad the Drill Sergeant

Taught us hand to hand combat

Jump, tuck and roll

Three tours in Viet Nam

Radio broadcaster in Saigon.

Sisters say he got tired

By the time I arrived,

Not the best father

Not always kind.

Did everything he said

Much easier to do as told,

Learned from my sisters

Not to step out of line.

I may be his favorite

Baby of the family,

Learned to please my dad

To earn his time.

Ain't no free lunches

A father who picked cotton,

Taught his girls fortitude

Viet Nam Lessons.

The baby is the youngest

Lessons learned from watching,

To be the favorite,

Had to be molded.

Soldiers for daughters

Spit shine his boots,

Ready for combat

We knew the rules.

Stories he told us

About literacy and cotton

Listen to daddy

He has important lessons.

Daughters his favorites

Not one of us to spare

We have different memories

His daughters his soldiers.

FATHER'S DAY

June has a special day

Dedicated to Dad,

Most important voice

Strong and baritone,

Man of the home.

Funny guy

Makes fun of everyone.

Likes his sports,

Comes to every game.

Shows up when needed

Cheers us on.

Lifts us off our feet

Twirls us around.

Dad cuddles his wee ones

Father, man of God.

Shares his stories

Loves our mom.

Shows us what a dad should be

He cares for mommy,

Holds her hand

Makes her happy.

Father is the real man

Example of what can be.

Sets the standard

For future men.

MOST IMPORTANT VOICE

Dad

The most important voice in my life

Rough and direct

Always listening

Always right.

Now I am older

Understanding your 'why',

Compassion for your life

Directing me with your voice.

Never telling me wrong,

Ever so right.

I listened as a child,

To the most important voice in my life.

POOR

When you are poor and don't know it

Holes in your shoes

Same pair of trousers

Five days a week.

Eating rabbits and fishing

The normal way of life.

Picking cotton for a living

Cuz it's the 1930's,

And your dad can't read or write.

As if you knew any better

Living in a tent.

Teachers knew your vulnerabilities

Poorest kid in the class,

Or so you thought

As the ruler smacks your hands.

Aunt Faye to the rescue

Standing six feet tall,

Did not take anyone's bullying

Gave a talking to the staff.

Just because you don't know it

Being poor and all,

Gives nobody the right

To punish and demean

A small boy

For being poor.

BISCUITS AND GRAVY

I love buttermilk biscuits,

Gravy too.

Some grits on the side

Fried eggs and bacon

Makes a family meal

Just like mom would do.

As we all gathered around

Stealing bits of bacon

Out of the pan.

Dad at the head of table

Kids and grandkids all around

Praising mom.

Breakfast binds us together

Praying at every meal

Mom's cooking always the best.

If stranded on an island

Along with the sand,

I'd only pray for biscuits and gravy

And my mom holding my hand.

ALL THE GLARING
RED FLAGS

I THOUGHT

Thinking things would get better

I saw it like I was,

Shattered lenses

Perspective just broken.

Apologize to myself

Forgiven the shame,

Thinking it would get better

Didn't understand,

My dreams of better

Didn't make it right.

Broken lenses

Didn't make it right

Didn't make it wrong.

Pain became a distant memory,

Remembering me

Remembering you.

You were a destroyer

My lenses were broken.

Thinking it would get better

Thinking it was normal

To struggle through the bad

Always remembering the good.

Sometimes letting go

Meant my lenses were not broken.

I knew it would not get better

Could not get better

So, I chose

Then I left.

RED FLAGS

Done this before

Tried this before

Yeah, I am no quitter

For sure.

Ignoring red flags

Ignored them before

Maybe the third time is the gem

Yeah, I'm not quitter

For sure.

At least I am consistent

Rationalizing the lesson

Repeating the same

Seems to be comfortable

For sure.

Something tells me it can be different

Red flags flaring

Learning the lesson is the reason

I keep returning for more

For sure.

I'M WITH STUPID

Diminished capacity

Unwilling to grow

Prefers what he thinks he already knows.

Normal is living off the dole

Motivation lacking

He will get it right in the afterlife.

Wants to be a leader and a teacher

Savior of souls

He comes from the Shankill Road.

He just doesn't get it

Not expecting much

To dream would be beyond his comprehension

Because he might actually need to take action.

He doesn't expect much

Keeps him small that way.

His truth keeps him down

But that is where he chose to stay.

Let's others pick up his mess

Don't agree with his warped doctrine

He has to be right

To condone his holiness.

MISSED THE BOAT

When several life rafts were offered

In raging waters, you still waited for the boat,

As if the boat was your only solace.

Friends proffering hands

Instead of choosing help,

As if you were used to throwing away the best chances.

Your drowning was more important than surviving

The struggle like a Brownie girl ribbon across your chest.

Instead of winning buttons and badges

You chose the struggle.

Bewildered with your life

Never understanding your choices.

The life rafts you never accepted,

Blaming the boat and no second chances.

BOOZE THE DESTROYER

Nicest guy on the planet

Easy on the eyes

Likes his beer nightly

All a disguise.

Cuz once he hits the hard stuff

Straight without coke

He gets mean and belligerent

His mask was his guise.

Fools you until he's got you

As in 'no way out',

Trapped in a cycle

You thought would work out.

Threatens and intimidates

Cuz he's really scared

You might leave him

Then he'd have to fool another.

Grabs you buy the throat

Wants to give you black eyes

To show off at work

Hey, no big surprise.

He will demean your success

Blame you and everyone else

Cannot see he is the problem

Smarter than everyone else.

Thinks he is in control

Booze and all,

Cuz he cannot control his addiction

From the Jekyll and Hyde.

Change the locks sister

Pack his bags.

Kick him to the curb

He is just trash.

Make sure the cops are there,

So he doesn't beat your ass.

SPREADSHEET

Keep a record

Of all my dates

On an excel spreadsheet

Keeping track of so many one liners.

No wonder they are not married

So many alike

Looking for Farrah

But, drive a pedaled motor bike.

Thinking they are God's gift

Impervious to their flaws

Premature ejaculation

Cannot keep it hard.

Spreadsheet tells a story

Facts do not lie

Adding up the math

Maybe, a four or a five.

Bald and big belly

Hairs in their nostrils

Eyebrows all bushy a mile high

Never a trim cuz they are blind.

So much confidence

For a man that leaves tracks

Doesn't wash his hands

And still shits his pants.

Owes the IRS money

Survives on social security

Brags about his penis size

Scheming to spend my money.

Think they deserve a younger chick

Never their own age

Narcissistic behavior

Complains about his ex

How she ruined his life.

Spreadsheet is there to remind me

Should have married Mike

He was the best choice

He was Mr. Right.

One-hundred dates later

Took me eleven years.

So many Mr. Wrongs

Repeating the same behavior.

Analysis has proven

Spreadsheets don't lie

Better to be single

Than to settle for Mr. Why.

YOU

You stole my youth

Now when you are ready to die

I cannot help but wonder

Why I bother

Why do I cry?

When you were so cruel

And words rough

No time for any others

Solitude your only profession.

Could not be bothered with someone else's soul,

Now you are dying

Who is going to tell your story?

Will you ever wonder

What you could have done differently?

How you could have made a difference?

If you had only softened your heart…

But, you kept your heart all to yourself

Truth be told.

Maybe your heart

Was not worth sharing

The way you wanted it

The way you intended.

No need to be understood

Just like the gunner on the helicopter in Viet Nam

You played your life with unlimited odds.

Black cowboy hat

Dusty boots

You rode your horse

Like it was your homecoming.

Comfortable in the saddle

You thought you could cowboy up.

Your boots outlasted you.

Suck it up.

And your cowboy hat now hangs alone,

And you are gone.

You'll never wear that cowboy hat where you are going

Because you couldn't share your heart.

YOUR APPROVAL

Your approval needs no respect

I would not depend

Even if you were heaven sent.

Nor does it matter

Your thoughts of me,

Earth shattering news

Would not prevail.

Your condescension

Distain for a voice,

Moves nothing in my heart.

Two shits I would not give.

Deserving of no response

Enough not needed to be said.

My opinion of you

I left for dead.

AGENDA

Only time gives answers

Rushing yourself along

Full stop on headstrong

What I think, what I want.

Slowing down for sanity

Instead of breaking the waves

Helps me turn off the tape recorder

Rewinding the reset.

So easily caught up in excitement

Thrill of one more maybe.

Potential is only revealed

As his agenda unreels.

Take time for distance

Never rushing the score,

Friend or foe

Eventually, comes to the door.

Until he shows up

Ready to reveal his core,

He will hide behind the curtains

Showing you speed is his norm.

What you want

Speeding right along,

May not be your destination.

Just a detour

To teach you he isn't for sure.

EGO

Ego whispers into my ear

Fear, fear, fear

Ego compels.

You are right

You must be right.

Ego is contractual.

I will love you more when

You grab onto my propaganda.

Ego passes judgment,

Judgment all about me.

Ego whispers harshness,

Harder and harder on me.

Ego despises change,

Personal growth ego's nemesis

Believing you are big

But ego makes you small.

Ego lacks humility

No turn of the other cheek

Fight back with badness.

Sink to the ego level,

Ego does not give an inch.

Self-serving and all about me

Drives fear into attachments.

Ego is unforgiving,

Hooked on unhealthy bitterness

Damages intimacy

Keeps score in relationships.

Ego destroys,

All that you are

All you love about yourself,

Puffs you up

False sense of identity.

Ego punishes boundaries,

Pushes you to compel

Ego's fear drives and pushes the pedal

Convinces the warped view is reality.

Ego is the devil in you.

GOTCHA

She acts demure and defenseless

Plays a tight game.

While you come to her rescue

Provide her protection.

Plays the victim with her eyes downcast

What once was meek and docile

Has turned to quicksand.

She has your balls

Now in her hands.

You fell for it

Hook, line and sinker.

So feminine and subservient

Stroking your ego,

Bows to your wishes

Subverts her real intent.

You would rather be manipulated

By some poon tang

By some little thang

Cuz she strokes your manhood

And that little brain.

Why not a partner

One who is your equal,

Who you can respect

And call her your 'ME-QUAL'.

Afraid of a real woman

She challenges your senses,

She isn't below you

You consider her a threat.

She is your equal

Stands her own ground

That is not your preference.

Cannot handle a real woman

Who speaks her mind,

She might cause friction

You might have to grind.

Her respect you must earn

Work hard for her affection

You would rather be lazy

And not deal with her smarts.

She might out success you

She might be competition

She will not bow down

Stroke your ego

She won't excuse your omissions.

SHAME

Shame, blame, and belittling

A cycle of abuse.

You think you are better than the rest of us

Too big for your britches.

Messages are clear

A good tongue lashing

Put you into your place

Forever imprinted on your DNA.

Genetic code for shame

Naughty girl

Annoying girl

You deserve what you get.

Judgment embedded to last a lifetime

Cruelty meant to emotionally cripple

Abuse cycle recurring daily

If not in person, in your mind.

Family is a detriment to finding your value.

Tape recorder to turn off!

Thoughts to relearn

Make these thoughts new and loving

Kindness and compassion

And light my way.

GENETIC DYSFUNCTION

A cycle of dysfunction

Twelve generations strong

Permeates our cells

Telling us we are wrong.

Denies freedom to happiness

Aching, persistent pessimism

Steals happy memories

Makes us feel unworthy of love.

Cynical and irrational

A silent destroyer

Lives in our homes and culture

Passing to our children.

Impairs our vision

Guilts our conscience

Soul destroying negative surroundings

Decaying our joy.

Correcting the cycle

Switching ourselves on

Takes years of recognition

Building proper boundaries

Fixing our shaken souls.

INEVITABLE

Inevitable outcome

Even though we know

When he cares

He shows.

Excuses for his behavior

Convenient to understand

Still we return

To feel rejection again.

While others warn us,

We keep an open heart

Instead of moving on

Still cling to the inevitable.

Endure humiliation and shame

Because we keep going back

Instead of grasping

We should value ourselves more.

Nobody can tell us

Until we finally understand

Truth is in our value

The standard we prevail.

Accepting poor behavior

No reciprocity and total disrespect

An indicator to cut our losses

Leaving him in the distance.

LOVE THEM BOYS

DENNIS

Retired now

Hard working soldier

Did time in the desert

Away from home.

Mamas adore your presence

Children appreciate their dad

Friends call you Dos

To me you are …

simply the man that can.

Treasured grandson

Favorite brother

You can do it all

All with pleasure.

Loves to please

Worried to let you down.

Avoiding the disappointment

Still doing all he can.

My friend is a lover

Silent in his affections.

Would rather show you

Than tell you

A man of his word.

Parts of his anatomy are sensitive

Just like his ego.

So let him show the way

And maybe he will stay.

As long as he can handle

The space between

The woman who loves him

Who calls him friend

And his other demands.

NOT MEANT TO BE

He was my first and only

Never to replicate

Could never match the chemistry.

Never the same after twenty-nine

Seems long ago

Not a distant memory,

Just a sliver of time.

Each decade in passing

Years we would go,

Recognized you from behind

In Vegas and Costco.

Introductions to family,

Memories disturbed.

I felt the pangs of loss

My heart to unload.

Sobbing for days,

Twenty years ago,

Feels like yesterday

Tossing my sorrow,

Letting it go.

Time to move on.

Thirty years ago.

My sleep still disturbed

My heart recalls.

Cries for the memories

Nothing to compare

The man of my dreams

Left in despair.

Once I cherished,

Guess it was meant to be,

For you to search your path

And me to find me.

I know you remember

Not long past

Maybe it means more to me

Each time we pass.

When we see each other

Chemistry still there,

Know my love for you

Compresses the air.

Not meant to be.

Our paths will cross

Briefly each decade

To remind me

Our time

Will never come to pass.

FAST BOYS AND FAST CARS

Just a girl

I like 'em fast

Three, two-barrel carburetors

'69 GTO got my attention.

Goin' on a date

That car

Could eat anything on the road

Fast boy and his fast car

His Pontiac was so good lookin'.

'71 Firebird was just my style

4-barrel 455 engine

Could do donuts around the school yard

Down on the pedal.

Dating two boys

With two fast cars

Can't decide which one to marry

Depends on the color of the car.

Dad says I don't need to decide

Just enjoy the ride

Crusin' down the boulevard

A boy on each side.

CHASING BOYS

So, boy crazy

I like their backs

Butts from behind

Shoulders all wide and arms to match.

Gotta catch 'em when they're blind

Can't see what's in front of them

Cuz they have a one-track mind

I'm a girl on a mission.

Tall and blond

Thighs of steel

Looks good in 501s and a uniform

From the back of course.

He may not speak my language

Being foreign and all

But his back and shoulders

Make me crawl.

Rubbing my hands on those thighs of steel

Turning him over

Shoulders appeal

Attacking his blindness.

Forget his lips

What matters is behind

Taking care of business

I'll take my time.

LATIN LOVER

Never thought I'd say it,

but boy is it true

Those Latin men have it going on

Taking their time.

May not speak English

Like me and you

But love has no language

When he's taking his time

Sends me to the moon.

Never would have thought

A man and his Latin genes

So skilled and whatnot

Making happy.

No words can describe

He can go for hours

Taking his time.

SUNDAY

A day of rest

Wake up refreshed

To sleep in

Catch my breath.

Blueberry pancakes

Fresh from the griddle

For me and you

To share in the middle.

Sunday is our fun day

As we play together

Sheets tangled in the mess

And bless each other

Kisses on my neck.

Time with you

Sharing breakfast

My one day a week

To nestle in our nest.

Squeeze you so tightly

I never want to forget

Sunday with the man of my dreams

Utter content.

Sweet tea on the porch

Afternoon delight,

You make my morning

Evening, noon, and night.

KISSES

I like a snuggle and a cuddle

Spooning real tight

Kisses on the nape

Of my lower neck.

Wrap your arms around me

From behind

Let me feel your heartbeat

Your kisses

They abound.

Lay down beside me

Let me feel your breath

As you send tiny kisses

All over my neck.

Gently fold me

With your hands to my back

As I touch your muscles

From your chest to your hip.

Connected by skin

Sharing each breath.

THE DIP

That dip in his abdomen

The one that starts at his hip

Right along his six pack

Yep, that dip in his hip.

In 501s unbuttoned

Lowered just enough

To glimpse his glory

The dip that drives my flurry.

Touch it

Thumbs down the crevice

Fingers digressing

A woman can appreciate.

When he steps out of the shower

No towel intended

Makes me smile

And get all flustered.

Can't even speak

No words to describe

His magic dip

Glorious man.

HUMAN
CONDITION

MY FRIEND

My friend is a beacon

Showers me with light.

Showing me direction,

And guiding through dark.

My friend is the hornet

Stings me with her fight.

Tasking my frustration

Turning all to right.

My friend is the fire

Blue lights up the night,

Orange flakes of flicker

Warming my soul to bright.

My friend is causation,

Holding my hand so tight,

Walking with me

Facing my biggest fright.

My friend is forever,

Never letting me go.

Throughout the years

Only my best friend truly knows.

MY FRIEND LYNN

My friend,

She used to be a namby-pamby.

Now she tells it like it is

Like it is going to be.

My friend,

She used to be so quiet,

Now she speaks it like it is

Like it has to be.

My friend, Lynn

She used to be so calm,

Now she calmly tells it like it is

Not in a calm way.

My friend,

She got some guts.

She got some tough.

She opened her mouth

She learned to speak in the rough.

ALL I CAN HANDLE

When I've had all can handle

And I'm strong because I have to be,

Not because I want to be.

The strength comes from somewhere

Somewhere I thought I would be.

The struggle and the strength

Illusive and unknown,

From the depths of my gut

I trudge along.

Somewhere in the unknown.

Sometimes I wonder

Wonder where it goes,

Time to struggle

Time to not know,

Somewhere in the time

I learned to let go.

GENDER ROLES

Traditional gender roles

Ghost of the past

Changing dynamics

Living in contradictions.

Labels once suited

Have passed.

Equality in gender

Still breaking the glass.

Dealing with fragile egos

Old men eventually pass.

Requires a different generation

Women rising,

Challenging the status quo.

Whether she chooses

To make money

Or be domestic Goddess,

Most important work

Is always in the home.

Women are doing it

Most of us, alone.

Serving two functions

Struggling for personal success

Fulfilling the needs

Of everyone in the nest.

Nurturer and provider

Balancing our roles.

Tasks are equal

While creating a home.

Perspective is crucial

Similar goals

Sharing responsibility

We each have a role.

Caring for each other

Meeting personal goals

Fulfilling desires

In office and home.

AGGRESSIVE WOMAN

Media and Hollywood like to portray

Strong women as bitches

Dykes and lip stick lesbians.

Fat chicks with attitudes,

Aggressive and manly,

Attributed to her success.

She couldn't do it on her own

Had to suck some ****

To achieve her position.

You just can't admit

She is your best competition.

Really quite irritating

A woman of intelligence

Has to explain her success.

You call her aggressive and pushy

A man would be called assertive

A pat on his back

He is a 'go getter'

Fast track to management.

She scares your manly

Trips you up

Call her names

Soothes your ego.

A woman has two jobs,

Works twice as hard

Breast feeds her wee ones

Makes sure her house is tidy.

Fighting for her life

She deserves it all

Comes at a price.

Strong and capable

Smart to boot

Has to make it his idea

So, he gets all the credit.

Referred to as the bitch

Cuz she won't tolerate disrespect

As if that is some hurtful label

One she won't regret.

MY VOICE

Please do not edit my voice

My voice is all I have

Expresses my memories

Impresses my desires.

Please remember my voice

I come from a place of experience

Sharing my deepest thoughts

Impresses my vulnerability.

Please understand my voice

The deepest parts of me

Explaining my struggles

Impresses my expression.

Please appreciate my voice

My unique set of life alterations

When you edit my voice

You diminish your capacity to listen.

DUAL ROLES

I pulled double duty

Fulfilling both roles

Now to celebrate both days

Mother's Day and Father's Day.

My daughter

Only child

Dad barely present

Another family consumed his attention.

Encouraging her to reach out

To be the bigger person

To sustain a bit of connection

Supportive mother role.

She learned boundaries,

Not to accept his distance.

How to separate her worth

From his absence.

Into adulthood

She still feels his unacceptance

As if

His guilt keeps him distant.

He projects his emotions

Knows he did wrong.

Somehow daughter still suffers

From his absence.

In death

He will find

A certain kind of sadness

And uniquely qualified

To feel the pain.

YOU SAY, I SAY

You say I am a strong woman,

You say I am an independent woman,

You say I am a capable woman,

You say I am an aggressive woman.

I say I have nobody else to rely on but myself.

I say I have learned to be strong from setbacks.

I say I am resilient because I had to be steadfast.

I say I am assertive because there was

And is no softer way.

I say I am capable because there is no other alternative.

I say I am unstoppable because there was no other way to move

But forward

I say I am strong because,

Only me and my dreams to pursue.

You say, I say.

When we say,

Together

We light the way.

A unique challenge

Alone in this life.

Sometimes plans do not always make the woman,

Instead

The resilient woman makes the plans.

Plans of vision, a singular event

Alone is sometimes the hard part.

ZERO REGRETS

Zero regrets

That is my motto

Doctorate in screw ups

More to follow.

Take courage

Nothing to fear

Laugh at yourself more often

Learn from my example.

Jump in the mud

Spread it all around

Every nook and crevice

Rub it up and down.

Gotta' get some dirty

See life through

Make a mess

Hit the blues.

Waiting at the turnstile

Never having the right change

Jumping the railing

Flailing in pain.

Take the journey

Mud pits and all

One day you'll tell a story

Handcuffed to a stall.

Life has no meaning

Without sharing your story,

God sent you blessings

No regrets to postpone.

Never falter in your courage

To muck it all up

Your story is the lesson

Mud faced and all.

REJECTION

Rejection-

Don't take it personal

More about you than me

The worst thing that can happen

You …

Have set me free.

Like asking for a second date

If the first one did not go so well

No need to repeat

Chemistry just not there.

What I have to offer

May not be your style

But, suits me perfectly

I will continue to smile.

No need to explain

Two paths not meant to cross.

We can agree on that.

Take your iterations

And shove them up your ass.

TESTICULAR FORTITUDE

Stepping up

Into that ring

Fast ball gonna hit you

If you do not take that swing.

I will not tolerate you

If you cannot join the team

We are either on the same page

Or you are out of my league.

My balls sit on my chest

Not hiding away

I got the gumption

As I step up to bat.

You either meet your obligations

Bring home the fat

Keep yourself honest

Or get out of the way.

No time for losers

Liars in the wake

Treat me like your woman

Defend my name.

Respect my spirit

Fight for my honor

Stand up and be counted

Your balls full swing.

My daddy taught me

To not settle for less

If you lack testicular fortitude

You won't pass my test.

SO I DID

Started life over

So I did

Difficult times ahead.

Got past your voice in my head

So I did

Recurring messages

Messages I learned to dread.

Got to be free

So I did

Time to dream again

Space to discover myself.

Got to feel good again

So I did

Feels so good

To do it all over.

My spirit came alive

So it did

Opportunity to start all over

Time to shine my light

Again.

YET AGAIN

One more go

On my own

Seems to be the only way

The only answer I know.

Comfortable in confusion

Comfortable on my own

Seems to be the only way I go

The only answer I know.

Effortlessly practiced

Becomes my norm

Seems to be the only way I go

The only answer I know.

Forget to breathe

In the pause

Sometimes holding my breath

The only breath not to breathe.

Took years to get here

Years to understand

The only way to go

Was to follow the unknown.

LIGHT

If you're feeling pretty shitty

And really kind of low

Weather is super gloomy

Ruining the flow.

Take a bit of inventory

Don't let bitterness ruin your go

Try to stay enlightened

Understand your mo-jo.

Dark clouds impending

Umbrella for shelter

Protecting your spirit

Keep pushing mo'.

Dark clouds will filter

Soon you will know

Your thoughts are only temporary

Let them go.

Say a little prayer

Let lightness fill the air

Feel your attitude changing

Nothing more to despair

SWING

Hit it

Out of the ballpark

Watch it go.

Put my back into that swing

Connected bat to ball,

Never a doubt.

Because in life

If you don't step up,

The curve ball is going to hit you

So, step out of the way.

But don't lay that bat down,

Until you've exhausted your swings.

BUCKET LIST

My bucket list expired

Dreams dried up, retired

Now I spend time

Working on my fuckit-list.

Lost my temper

Not so cool

Tongue lashed out

Spitting and drool.

Getting tired of bucket-list remorse

Tubing down the river

Golfing the course.

Gotta be something better

Besides waking up to stutter

Can't explain flaking out

Bucket-list items just clutter.

New fuckit-list items

Feels so good

Knowing there is potential

Not expecting much

Just changed the title.

Now with delight

My fuckit-list surprises

Not giving a shit

Taking pride in my progress.

ALL THAT IS ME

Folly in choices

Now in later years

Return to my decisions.

Learning the hard,

Was the only way.

Lessons uniquely mine

Resilience to the core

Expressions of the journey

Crooked and unknown

Diversions plenty.

To do it any other way,

Never could have happened.

To be all that is me

What a masterpiece…

As I rock back and forth

Perspective anew

Enjoying the view.

ALREADY

Already written

Nothing left to say.

Ideas proliferated

Pontificating the same.

Talking heads

Bobbing a'top the waves

Meaningless words

As if something to say.

Nothing to inspire

Just making noise

Scuttling up fear

Mucking in the mire.

Make it worthwhile

Time well spent

Listening to your diatribe

Words need to make sense.

Tell me something simple

A new way to think

Help me experience

Travel your path.

And learn..

Of your struggles

Something I haven't had.

Show me the new way

Different from the rest

Something never written

Something never said.

RECONCILE

Time has come

Reconcile my past,

Put it all behind me

Let is pass.

Foraging forward

Scorching my path,

Leaving behind

What didn't serve me.

No time like the present

Lit the match.

Never looking back

Because back doesn't serve me.

Only plan that matters

Guiding my life,

Is the resounding knowing

Only I can make it right.

Not that life gets easier

But, at least I know the signs,

Of struggle, endurance and compassion,

Showering my soul,

Walking in the light.

Because I lit the match

Torched useless memories,

Seared in their wake,

Creating better eternities,

Choosing better mistakes.

CHANGE

Uncomfortable and uncertain

Easier to stay the same

Return to familiar situations

Compromising

Is not change.

Facing myself

Hardest part of change

Acknowledging my needs

Refusing to do

What serves me best.

Cuz that takes courage

Out in the open

Releasing control

Returning to familiar

Is easier than the unknown.

Listening is the toughest part

Like a dog rolling in stench.

Revisiting the refuse

Is what I know best.

Situation has to be untenable

Wits end.

To drive me forward

To make amends.

What makes me vulnerable

Makes me strong

Builds courage

Righting the wrongs.

Only obstacles standing in my way

Are my thoughts about change.

So much easier to stay

And be miserable

Complaining

Driving friends away.

Necessity is my forward

Driving me to change.

Following my radiator cap

No need to look back.

Cuz I got this…

Under control.

A life I call sacred

Is mine to switch up.

Leave behind the rubbish

And listen to my soul.

Change was my enemy

Now I relish

Uncertain and uncomfortable

My u-turns in life.

I listened

Didn't return

To the stench

I called a previous life.

BAD DIRECTIONS

When life gives you bad directions

Hard to find the right path

Listen to your gut

That voice trying to connect.

Take life in small doses

Always search for a higher thought

Because in this moment

Being all 'here'

Is all you've got.

Directions guide

Sometimes bad advice

The straight and narrow

Was not your ride.

Took several detours

Living with diversions

Potholes and flat tires

Nobody to the rescue.

Take those bad directions

Turn them upside down

Now your angels

Can show you diversions.

Assisting with better directions

Compass pointing the path

Stars for guidance

Still needing the map.

Trusting your gut

Angels to the rescue

You decided to listen

Found your way back.

FLUNKED THIRD GRADE

Held back in third grade

While friends carried on

Held back with shame

Did not understand repercussions

Refusing to read for my teacher

Teacher shame.

Forgot her name long ago

Principal wanted to teach me a lesson

Obstinate children could not progress

He and teacher made sure I understood

The silent treatment and refusing to read

Punished for obstinance.

Mrs. Cooper summer school tutor

Taught me to erase with an eraser

Got me up to speed

Had no issues with my reading abilities

Could read Zane Gray just as well as she.

Parents did not fight back

Bullied to obedience just like me

Refusing to read for that witch of a teacher

Demons held me back.

SQUIRRELLY

He's a squirrelly dude

Darting to and fro

Can't make a decision

Which way to go.

He buries his acorns

A nest in the tree

Waiting for winter

He saved for his needs.

His neighbor found an apple

Fallen freshly from a tree

Was a bit sour

Ate to the core.

He and his neighbor

Not two alike

Squirrelly one and squirrelly two

Became best of buds.

Frolicking friends

One saves and one don't

Differences abounding

Never any heed

When one has more

Shares with one in need.

Two squirrelly dudes

Loving their trees

Because friends forever

Are friends indeed.

BAD DRIVER

Fast lane driver

Doin' 65

Smokin' something

Must be high.

Obstructing a mile of traffic

Brake lights are red

Keeps pressing on her brake

Because she can't stop talking.

Passenger's feet on the dashboard

Yacking away

Seats all reclined

Enjoying their day.

They must live on some other planet

Taking their time

While the rest of us are distracted

Avoiding their crime.

Dip shit central

Want to wring those necks

Impeding the flow of traffic

I bet she's reading a text.

The rest of us flip the bird

As blood pressure increases

Wondering why

Their '82 Honda isn't in pieces

Ain't no granny driving that car

Just some selfish chick

Blind to her flaw

She should be in the slow lane.

Big Dodge Ram

Riding her rear

She's flickin' her doobie

Lit and all

These two ain't Cheech and Chong

No destination or job to avoid

Just her pal and a doobie

Impeding the flow.

Major pet peeve

Go fast and make it last

If you are slow

Stay in your lane.

AUGUST ALREADY

What happened to the year?

We long for Spring and budding flowers

Then summer is near

Swimming, picnics and the 4th of July

Summer monsoons and dust storms

Then August flies by

Trick or treating and costume fun

Up and down the street.

We plan for Thanksgiving

Turkey, mashed potatoes, yams, gravy and splendid treats

Those pies are so delicious

Hoping to avoid family arguments

Not talking politics or religion

Dinner as a family

Enjoying mom's cooking.

Then we decorate our trees with gifts at bottom

Lights are on to remember why we celebrate

Christmas music plays

The special day

To open the gifts and give thanks

For the pleasure.

Then New Year begins

And here we go again

Each cycle ends before it begins.

To live in each moment

And not look forward to the Spring, the blooms, the summer

Seems to go so fast

As we look back

Just day after day

And what we have to remember

Are the moments.

ON THE I-10

A lonely stretch

Drive it all by myself

14 hours of high desert and sand storms

Me and Tom Petty travel together

"Cuz it's a long, long road".

Phoenix to Lordsburg covered with cops

Got a speeding ticket

Paying some road tax

91 in a 75 way to fast.

Once I hit El Paso

Only eight hours to go

Speed limit is 80

Hittin' cruise control.

El Paso takes an hour from end to end

Then to Van Horn

Ft Stockton is just an hour or so

Heading for the hill country.

Wildflowers still blooming

Blue Bonnets galore

Blues and yellows

Blanket hill country floor

Can't wait for some good BBQ

Home to San Anton.

NOBODY KNOWS

Nobody knows

Nobody cares

Sparkle on your own.

Solutions will follow

Answers will come

Just take a step forward

Into the unknown.

The only opinion that matters

Is the one you call your own

Take joy in repercussions

Even when you fail.

Resources are plenty

Personal trial and error

This journey is yours

Ever mindful of however.

Speak to your wisdom

Only way to find answers

Is when you travel the course

And find

The only opinion that matters is your own.

FRAGILE ME

MAKE A DECISION

Make a decision

Stick to it

And do it well.

Not looking back

Straight ahead and determined

My decision is the path.

Make it quick

After careful consideration

When I doubt, I wait it out.

One decision

Changes everything

Creates the steam.

Pushes me forward

Keeps me on path

You taught me to make the decision.

I stuck to the path

I fuel the steam.

APPRECIATION

Appreciation

Starts with appreciate

And takes action,

Sharing genuine reciprocity.

Simple as ABC

Easy to declare

Hard to pull teeth,

If it just isn't there.

Not to be taken for granted

Sharing the love

Moving the vocal chords,

Sounding out the words.

The love of appreciation

Begins with gratitude

To share often and genuinely,

Kindness clearing the path.

Appreciate with goodness

No malice to poison our hearts

Starts with gratitude

To lighten each other's dark

FEELING INSPIRED

One moment at a time

One breath at a time

Calming my mind

Breathing in what I desire

Breathing out what I no longer require.

Allowing what I didn't know I needed

To approach

Only thoughts to prosper

Replacing what didn't serve me

Higher level thinking

Higher level believing

Begins with a breath.

Feeling inspired

Starts with desire.

STORM

Storm cuts the path

Bullies through my veins

Preparing me for better.

Quiet moments

Ponders my mind

Reaching for solace

Wishes left behind.

Turning off the tape recorder in my head

Stillness

Billowing clouds overhead

Sparkles flicker, showering down.

Touching stars,

Dog, Olive by my side

At peace in my space

Calming the storm

Shutting down the race.

Just a few moments of my own

Today I slow down

Storm at my own pace

Letting go to create a better space.

WHENEVER

Whenever comes to naught

And nothing left to spare

I ask for direction

Sometimes direction never comes.

Whenever comes to naught

And nothing left to spare

I search for answers

Sometimes answers never come.

Whenever comes to naught

And nothing left to spare

I find myself waiting

Sometimes waiting never waits.

Whenever comes to naught

And nothing left to spare

I put my foot on the pedal

Sometimes moving keeps me from waiting.

Whenever comes to naught

And nothing left to spare

I find myself moving

Sometimes moving

Is the right direction.

THE MOST IMPORTANT

The most important parts of me

Dream to hope

Hope to dream

Still wishing.

The most important parts of me

Take the road

Not most trodden

Still treading.

The most important parts of me

Create a future

Knowing the future is there to be created

Still creating.

The most important parts of me

Trust the process

Knowing the process is not the destination

Still proceeding.

The most important parts of me

Knows 'the why' is the reason

Still knowing.

THIRTY SUMMERS

Thirty summers you asked if I had left

Just thirty summers

To complete the best.

A visual of each summer

Springs to mind,

Warm sun and bright sunshine

Stormont green and dogs running free.

Making the most

Thirty summers I have,

Monsoons to bring needed rain

Not all sunshine and flowers.

Imagining potential

My friend asked me the most important question,

Changed my life

Leaving behind my original comprehension.

Left everything behind

To begin 30 new summers,

Without any answers

Learning to dream again.

Ground shaking

Uncertainty prevailed

Trusting in a higher source

Summer by summer, slowly.

To say the journey to summer was challenging

Took Fall, Winter and Spring-

Many seasons changing

Thirty summers still ahead

Reinventing thirty summers.

(Credit to Kelleen Doyle Scott for asking me "What are you going to do with your 30 summers?"
Belfast, N. Ireland 2009)

I KNOW

I know I'm a dreamer

Still chose the dream.

I know I'm hopeful

Still chose hope.

I know I'm fearless

Still chose courage.

I know I'm unfiltered

Still chose the same words.

I'm God's imperfect creation

Still chose God.

Still I know,

Nothing at all.

ALL THAT MATTERS

All that matters

Anything with meaning

Starts with why

And continues with why not.

Rare, meaningful moments

Sudden glimpses of air

Fill my heart with gladness

Nothing left to spare.

Days begin with eternity

Eternity begins my day

Sharing the best moments

Brightness illuminates the way.

Snatching the why

Believing in why not.

YEARNING

Parts of my yearning

Parts of me, wholly imperfect, even flawed

Those intimate parts of me

Giving, sharing, expressing,

Courage to love the deepest parts of my imperfections

Compelled to love

Me.

Parts of my yearning

Deepest core, soulful moments

Cause me to wonder,

So much to mull through

Charity for myself

Mercy for my soul,

Mercy for me.

Parts of my yearning

Wishing it were true.

Believing in my power

Strength to see me through.

I believe, I believe, I believe

Because for me,

It is true.

DIRECTOR OF MY MIND

Time to direct my thoughts

Doesn't mean negative thoughts don't come to mind

I get to choose which thoughts to dwell

Which thoughts to dispel.

Familiar movie in the making

Reel after reel

Editing the good stuff

Creating my own film.

Thoughts come and go

Images of good and bad

No sense in hanging on to

Non-supportive staff.

I set the scene

Write the script.

Keeping what is good

Directing my thoughts

Producing an epic

A film that will last.

FLASHLIGHT METHOD

I have learned to question

My own thinking

To dispel any chance

My thinking may be warped.

I have learned to question

My own fears

To dispel any chance

My fears are unfounded and unreal.

I have learned to question

My own opinions

To dispel any chance

They may be omissions.

I have learned to question

My lifetime choices

To dispel any chance

They may be mistakes.

I have learned to question

Unfair assumptions

To dispel any chance

The messages are true.

I have learned to question

What I see

To dispel any chance

My lenses are discolored.

I am still learning to question

My questions

To dispel any chance

My answers are betrayed,

By shameful voices.

MORNING

Every morning

Begins with a dose of gratitude

Start the day right

In receptive mode.

Receive all blessings

No strings attached

In the right mindset

Gratitude is best.

Keep your mind happy

Only good thoughts

Best of feelings

Focus on what is right.

Control is an illusion

Meet your dreams

They already exist

In the uncontrollables.

All you need is YOU

Stay tuned to your soul,

Let joy light your journey

By letting go of control.

THIS MOMENT

I thought for a moment

But, the moment passed

An event that didn't last

Long enough to decipher

Real intent of time long cast.

I thought for a moment

But, the moment passed

Really all the love

Of love that didn't last.

Just a spare moment

Freeze in time

Caught a rare glimpse

A touch devine.

So, here I sit in the moment

A blip in time

Just a few minutes

Disclosing my mind.

Senses jolted

Making it last

The simplest moment

Time caught in repast.

WAKING UP

Woke up from a nap

Persistent thought in my head

So much to do

No time for bed.

Slowing down

Foreign thought

Forever on the back burner

Keep pushing on.

Then I hear the voice

Reminding me just for today

Make the change to mindfulness

Make change a choice.

Keep each moment

In it's very own place

Deliberately remember

Focus on the space.

Stay tuned in the now

This very moment in time

Breathe in for peace

Exhale to release

Imagine stars.

Sprinkling the skies

Lounging on a cloud

Touching each sparkle

Heavenly dogs by my side.

IN THE WEE HOURS

In the wee hours of the morning

Before sun starts to break

My soul takes a detour

And begins to wake.

In the stillness of the darkness

Inspiration creeps

Small gentle nudges

Begging for a listen

A voice, so to speak.

Just an hour or so each morning

Heeding the call

Pen and paper

Allowing the flow

Something wants to participate

To answer the call.

THE PORCH

A porch at sunrise

Begins the day

Best thinking is always in a rocking chair

Just like grandma used to do

Rocked her troubles away.

Solitude in nature

Hummingbirds at the feeder

Nature's way of clearing my head

Rushing of wind through trees

Just like my thoughts and memories.

Swinging on a porch swing

Porch at dusk

End to my day

A time to reflect

Say goodnight and begin afresh.

TRIBUTE TO TOM PETTY

Raised my child

On the road

T Tops off

CD on repeat

Nothing gets better

Sharing my music.

The call that morning

Took me by surprise

Sadness in your voice

As you told me he had died.

My breath seemed to leave all at once

As I heard the cd on repeat

The feeling of being on the road

Sharing Tom with you.

Each song I hear

Brings me to that place

As I hold my breath,

I remember.

Now on the road

I still listen to the years

I get to hear his voice

And remember I raised my child on his music

I raised myself on his tunes.

195
GOD'S FAVORITE CREATURES

A DOG

A dog is a special place

That implacable piece of our hearts

The binding that tells us forever

Is forever one piece of our hearts.

A dog is a friend, the familiar space

That occupies our love and seals that place.

Forever their love shines on our spirit

Comforts in the fro.

A friend to love and cherish,

Only a dog knows our soul.

PILLOW

The softest pillow

Greets my cheek

 A blanket to cover

My dog as she sleeps.

Napping is special

The older I get

Appreciating 20 minutes

Solace and rest.

In the heat of summer

Sweet tea at my breast

Cools me down

As I begin rocking

Dog at my feet.

Summer breeze in the midst

Sweet smell of jasmine and gardenia

Rustling in the trees.

Exploring this moment

Life at ease.

Moments and senses

Combined in a flash

My dearest wishes

Coming to pass.

To be one in harmony

This peace it can pass.

As long as I'm happy,

And my dog as company,

Together we stay

Enjoying each moment

The simple passing of each day.

COLLECTORS

My besties are collectors

Dogs and cats

Strays and woebegones

Ducks for grandchildren.

Makes me wonder

Friends for life

Maybe I'm a stray

Or just a woebegone.

No matter

I'm part of a collection

Friends for life

Three legged and deaf

Blind and bedraggled.

Pitiful to some

Treasure to others

Makes no difference

To the woebegone.

Collection of mishaps

Love to the less fortunate

Because capacity to be tender

A lovely trait.

Loving kindness

No heart turns away

A person in need

An animal to feed.

SIX PACK

A solid six-pack

Four dogs and two cats

Completing each other

Sharing snacks.

No dog beds for them

Only mommy's bed will do

Slumbering and snoring

A menagerie of fur

Keeping each other warm.

Do not disturb

Or move in bed

They'll raise their heads

My little corner of the bed.

Eccentric

Just like my mom

Never thought I'd see it

I've been her all along.

Four plus two and room to grow

Love for my 'kids'.

Bless with their unconditional love

Show the way

Never ending compassion.

Treats in the morning

A daily routine

Milk in the saucer

Biscuits and cream.

A six-pack makes me seven

Part of their pack.

OLIVE AND SCOUT

Olive runs in autumn leaves

Sniffing all the trees

As she finds muddy spots

For her friend, Scout.

So, Scout can roll and plunder

In mud bogs

She goes asunder.

While Olive stays on the sidelines

Running back and forth along the edge

Scout swims in the black bog

She smells really bad.

So, we wash her off before heading home

Olive in the lead

And Scout drying off

In the grass and leaves.

She rolls and rolls

Two happy dogs

Living a good life.

COUSINS ON THE FARM

Seven cousins

Doing their bit

Feeding mama cow

Her treasured alfalfa

Filling her water barrell

Down it goes.

Having her baby

Mango is her name

She likes to frolic

And chase the kiddos.

Little ponies

Painted water colors

Ribbons in their mane

Tails 'swishin'

Grandma Annie

Gets those horses moving

On the trail.

Raised on the farm

Animals galore

Summer breezes

Swimmin' in the fishin' hole

Swingin' from a tire in the tree

Letting go

Cousins on the farm

Sharing time together.

OLIVE LOVES THE BEACH

Olive darts from the car

She knows the beach.

Running as fast as she can go

She finds wet sand.

Water is pretty chilly,

In Helen's Bay Northern Ireland.

Nothing stops wee sausage dog,

Short legs trailing as fast as they can.

Exploring sand dunes and tundra

Feet hardly touch the ground.

Cuz she is running as fast

as her tiny legs can go.

With the ocean water ebb and flow

She may run slow.

Wind blows her floppy ears

But this little dog loves her fun.

Joy on the beach

Like she walks on water.

Climbing rocks

Exploring the unknown

As only a dog can feel

Pure happiness

As we let her roam.

About the Author

Skeeter Smith is an author and poet. An Army brat (Drill Sergeant's daughter), born and raised in Germany, the youngest of four daughters, and lived in Northern Ireland and China. She loves traveling, learning about diverse cultures and meeting interesting people. Skeeter holds a Bachelor of Arts in History from Arizona State University, and a Master of Business Administration. Working in the financial industry full-time, Skeeter must indulge her creative writing energies in her spare time. Still, her most important accomplishments are that of devoted single mother and grandmother of three.

Skeeter's poetry appeared in a Texas literary magazine. She is an award-winning short story author in San Antonio and an active member of writing guilds throughout the state. Skeeter is currently writing a series of five historical novels. Her first in the series, Nordic Girl, will be released in late 2026.

* 9 7 9 8 9 9 3 6 8 0 0 0 2 *